THE
TOOTH BOOK

THE
TOOTH BOOK

ALAN E. NOURSE, M.D.

617.6   8491
N

David McKay Company, Inc.
NEW YORK

Library of Congress Cataloging in Publication Data

Nourse, Alan Edward.
The tooth book.

SUMMARY: Discusses tooth care, tooth decay, dental
problems, orthodontics, and braces.
1. Teeth—Care and hygiene—Juvenile literature.
2. Teeth—Diseases—Juvenile literature. [1. Teeth—
Care and hygiene. 2. Teeth—Diseases] I. Title.
RK63.N68   617.6   77-5239

ISBN 0-679-20376-1

10 9 8 7 6 5

MANUFACTURED IN THE UNITED STATES OF AMERICA

Contents

THE
TOOTH BOOK

CHAPTER
1

The Tooth
That Lost the War

Imagine for a moment that it is a bitter winter night long ago, and you are one of a ragtag army of American Revolutionary soldiers, waiting for your commander to send you off on a dangerous mission. The night is Christmas Eve, the year 1776. You are camped on the banks of the ice-clogged Delaware River, and across the river to the north you can see the lights of the city of Trenton.

That city is your target tonight, but your morale is at its lowest ebb. Many battles in this war have gone badly for General Washington. Far from hearth and home, you are drenched to the skin, your teeth chattering. Across the river, toasty-warm Hessian soldiers at Trenton are in the midst of Christmas Eve revelry. Soon, you have heard,

(1)

your commander is going to order you to cross the icy river in boats and try to catch the Hessians by surprise.

Resigned to your fate, you wait for the order—but nothing happens. Finally, long past midnight, you hear that unexpected disaster has struck. There will be no attack on Trenton this Christmas Eve; General Washington has developed an agonizing toothache and cannot even get out of bed, much less lead his troops across the river. So you roll up in your frozen blankets for the night and wait for the General's toothache to go away.

Three days later the toothache has improved enough so that the attack can be made; but by then the Hessian troops are fresh and alert. Your army is driven back across the river in disarray, and a bitter turning point in the war has been reached. As General Washington's army continues to flounder, the British win the war and retain a firm grip on the thirteen American colonies.

Of course, you say, this story is ridiculous. General Washington did *not* have a disabling toothache that fateful Christmas Eve. His victory at Trenton was a giant step forward in the fight for American independence. But in a larger sense, perhaps our story is not so ridiculous after all. On that fateful night, George Washington did not have a sound tooth in his head. Years before the Battle of Trenton, and for years after it, the father of our country suffered from recurrent painful toothaches, broken and rotting teeth, and gums festering with infection. He was forced to wear crude wooden dentures in order to chew his food.

Indeed, it was something of a miracle that George Washington was *not* struck with a toothache on the eve of some crucial battle. For all his high position as an American leader, he knew of no way to stop the decay of his teeth. In his day, scientific dental care was unheard of. The causes of dental disease were unknown, and the idea of controlling or preventing tooth decay was beyond anyone's wildest dreams. In the long run, bad teeth may even have killed George Washington. When he died of a throat infection in 1799, it may well have arisen from diseased and infected teeth, gums, or jawbone.

The First Dentist

George Washington was certainly not the first person made miserable by diseased teeth, nor was he the first to suffer from lack of adequate dental care. Sometime back in the dim reaches of the past, long before human history was first written down, Ug the caveman had a similar problem.

Ug was getting along in years. He was almost eighteen, well beyond average life expectancy at the time, and his teeth were growing old along with him. Several had been knocked out during battle-ax fights with other cavemen. Others had been broken off by gnawing on hard nuts, seed pods, and bones. But now something new had occurred: a piece of a back tooth had crumbled away, leaving a gaping hole, and Ug suddenly had an intolerable toothache.

Day after day the toothache grew worse, until one day

Ug made a curious discovery. By taking a chunk of resinous gum from the trunk of a fallen tree and packing it into the hole in his tooth, Ug found he could relieve the pain, and even use the tooth for chewing again.

By modern dental standards, Ug's crude filling left much to be desired. It kept dissolving or falling out, so he had to replace it every two or three days. The pine oil in the resin was not as good a painkiller as a dentist would use today, and the filling did not stop the decay that would soon destroy the tooth completely. Even so, Ug's filling was a remarkable achievement: the first crude restoration of a decayed tooth, relieving pain and allowing continued use of the tooth. With this simple repair of a damaged tooth, Ug the caveman had become the first dentist in human history!

Toothworms and Treatments

Of course, we don't know for sure that Ug the caveman ever existed, nor do we know just when the first attempts were made to restore diseased teeth. But crude attempts at dentistry were commonplace in the ancient world by the time the earliest written records were kept. Egyptian scrolls dating back to 3700 B.C. discussed dental diseases and methods of treatment. One Egyptian jawbone, dating from 2900 B.C., was found by archeologists to contain two holes drilled through the bone, probably to drain a large pocket of infection that had formed under a first molar. By 2600 B.C., the Egyptian pharaohs had special physicians entrusted with the care and treatment of the royal teeth. Unfortunately, such dental care was not very effective. The great pharaoh Ramses II, who died around 1225 B.C., had missing teeth, decayed teeth, infected teeth, and infectious destruction of jawbone areas underneath his teeth, according to x-rays taken of his mummified head.

It is hardly surprising that the earliest dentists did so poorly in treating dental disease. They were almost totally ignorant of the cause of dental problems. Why would one tooth decay and crumble while a tooth right next to it remained perfectly sound? What caused the swelling and festering of gums around the teeth? Above all, what caused toothache, the most dreaded symptom of dental disease? According to one ancient theory, toothache was caused by the Toothworm, a special demon that took the shape of a worm and bored into teeth to take up residence inside. The Toothworm was thought to cause horrible toothaches and to chew away at the inside of teeth until they crumbled and broke.

Efforts to expel such demons have taken many picturesque forms over the centuries. Ancient Chinese treated aching teeth by wrapping them with tiny pieces of parchment on which prayers and incantations had been written. In Germany during the Middle Ages, it was believed that kissing a donkey would relieve toothache, while early dentists in other regions recommended biting off the head of a mouse. Even today some primitive peoples still believe in the Toothworm in one form or another.

The Birth of Dental Science

Although belief in the Toothworm persisted for thousands of years, more valid ideas about dental disease and treatment began to emerge, bit by bit. The ancient Etruscans, who lived in central Italy before the founding of Rome, learned how to make gold dental bridges—wirelike devices used to hold false teeth in place in the mouth. The great Roman physician Celsus, who practiced just before the beginning of the Christian Era, wrote about many kinds of dental problems, and even prescribed opium to help relieve toothache. About two hundred years later, a Greek physician, Claudius Galen, filled painful tooth cavities with soft, easily worked metals such as lead. During the Middle Ages, a variety of crude dental instruments were invented, including files and chisels used for "drilling" decayed teeth and plierlike forceps used for extracting teeth. Medieval paintings showed professional "tooth pullers" dressed in pointed caps and wearing necklaces of the teeth they had pulled.

Yet for all this, a good 90 percent of our knowledge of modern dentistry—and especially *preventive* dentistry—has arisen in the two hundred years since George Washington suffered from toothache and used spring-loaded wooden

dentures to chew his food. The wonder of modern dentistry is that so much has been learned in so short a time. The tragedy is that so many people today still suffer quite needlessly from the same dental diseases that George Washington did, when virtually all those dental problems today can easily and inexpensively be prevented or controlled.

The Role of Prevention and Control

If most dental problems can really be prevented or controlled today, why do so many people avoid the dentist until they have serious trouble with their teeth? There is no easy answer to this question. Part of the problem is ignorance. Many people know very little about their teeth and the kinds of diseases that can affect them. They don't realize that regular tooth brushing and flossing at home and regular visits to the dentist can help prevent trouble; they wait until a painful toothache drives them to a dentist, far too late to protect their teeth from damage or possible loss. Those people who do brush their teeth regularly too often settle for a slapdash 20-second brushing once a day—not enough to get their teeth really clean. And far too many others just don't brush at all because they don't really understand what such a bothersome chore accomplishes.

Another reason why many people avoid dental care is

(7)

plain, simple fear of the dentist. We think nothing of going to a physician for a regular checkup—but going to the dentist is another matter. We hate the thought of sitting for long periods in a tilt-back chair with our mouths open. We hate the idea of someone poking around in our mouths. We hate the dentist's sharp instruments, the antiseptic smell, the unfamiliar feeling of the scaler or vibrator working on our teeth. We dread the thought of the anesthetic needle. And even though common sense tells us that a regular visit to the dentist is for our own good, we tend to put it off as long as we possibly can. The great opportunity for preventive dental care is then lost.

Many young people have another excuse for avoiding the dentist: the fear of having to wear braces. It may seem to you that your teeth are fine, but the dentist looks in your mouth and says, "Your teeth are coming in crooked. They don't meet each other properly." The dentist finds that you're biting too far forward, or too far back, or too far to one side, and your teeth will have to be positioned properly. The next thing you know, your mouth is full of "hardware," your once-pleasant smile is obscured by a jungle of wires, shiny metal strips, hooks, loops, and rubber bands. You may even have an outside wire harness around your face. There you are, burdened with braces for two or three or four years. Of course, you realize that orthodontics—the process of tooth alignment—may be good for you in the long run, but meanwhile it may seem that you've been rendered instantly ugly. Your self-image—the way

you see yourself in your mind's eye—has been shattered, and like many others, you may feel that you have to give up speaking or smiling, just so your braces won't show.

Finally, there are those who just can't understand why they should go to the dentist when there's nothing wrong. As Ogden Nash once said, "Man has to go to the dentist to keep his teeth in good condition so that he won't have to go to the dentist." Yet experience tells us that to get along with less dental care in the long run we need *more* dental care in the short run—preventive dental care.

Most dentists today believe strongly in combating dental disease in every way possible. They know that an hour or two spent in a dental chair, once or twice a year when the patients are young, can spare them weeks and months of future reparative dental service.

In the long run, successful prevention of dental problems depends upon you more than your dentist. The dentist cannot do it by himself, and it's not even enough to sit passively in a dental chair at certain prescribed times. To make preventive dental care work, you need to know some key facts about the origins of your teeth, the kinds of dental disorders that can occur, and the simple, commonsense things that you can do to prevent these disorders. You need to understand enough about the proper care of the teeth *between* visits to your dentist so that the time you do spend in the dental chair is not wasted.

In the following chapters we will consider each of these points. In addition, since repair or correction of dental

(9)

abnormalities is sometimes necessary in spite of the most faithful program of prevention, we will consider some of the things dentists can do, when necessary, to correct dental disorders. You may never really enjoy dental appointments, but at least you will understand better what the dentist is trying to do and why. You may never learn to love your braces, but at least you will be able to understand why they are necessary and how they may save you distress and discomfort in later years.

CHAPTER
2

Fifty-two Teeth

How many teeth do you have right now? Chances are you can't say without stopping to count. Even when you count, your answer may differ from the next person's.

Throughout life, you have different numbers of teeth at different times. A newborn baby should have none at all, but all the same, a baby is sometimes born with one or two front teeth fully emerged. An adult who has more than thirty-two teeth at one time is a rare specimen indeed, and the Smithsonian Institution would like to have a look at his skull. A few of you may never have more than twenty-nine or thirty or thirty-one teeth at a time; some people never develop all their third molars, or "wisdom teeth." If you are still within the "tooth-growing" period of your life, from the age of six months to age twenty-one or so, the number of teeth you may have at any one time is anybody's guess; and if you are in the "tooth-losing" period of life, from the age of twenty-one on, you may have fewer teeth than you should because some have been lost.

If you develop all the teeth you normally should, you will enjoy the use of fifty-two teeth, in all, in the course of your life. These fifty-two teeth emerge in two separate crops: twenty deciduous or "baby" teeth in the first or *primary* crop and thirty-two "permanent" teeth in the second or *secondary* crop. There is a period of time when these two crops of teeth overlap, so that some of the second crop are coming in while some of the first crop are still hanging on. But at best, the first crop of teeth lasts only a few years and then falls out. The second crop can last a lifetime with help from you and your dentist.

Different creatures depend upon their teeth in different ways for different things. Timber wolves, for example, use their long, sharp canine teeth to cut the hamstring muscles of aging or wounded deer and bring them to the ground for dinner. The wild elephant, on the other hand, depends for its life on four huge molar teeth, two upper and two lower, with which to grind up the six hundred pounds of vegetation that it requires each day to stay alive. These molars, each one about one foot across and weighing from eight to ten pounds, are gradually worn down to the gum line and drop out, a process that takes about ten years. When this happens, another set of grinding molars emerges from the elephant's jaws to take their place. In all, the wild elephant has only six sets of these molars to last a lifetime. When the sixth set has been ground down and lost, the elephant can no longer eat and starves to death.

Human beings don't depend on their teeth to stay alive;

they are just an efficient aid in chewing food. But we do count on them for our pleasant appearance (something elephants don't have to worry about), and they are vitally important in helping us form the words of our spoken language, a feat that no other creature on earth can achieve. Our lives are vastly more comfortable if we can preserve our teeth for as long as possible.

The Shape of Teeth to Come

Before we consider when and how our teeth come in, we need to know the kinds of teeth we have and some of the terms that dentists use to describe them. The first kind are the *incisors,* or "cutting teeth," located in the front of the mouth. We have eight such teeth in each crop, four above and four below. These are flattened and slightly curved teeth with straight, narrow edges that slide across each other like the blades of scissors when we bite into something. The two incisors in the middle of each jaw are called the *central incisors.* Those on either side of the central incisors, top and bottom, are the *lateral incisors,* which are not as wide as the centrals.

In humans the upper central incisors are noticeably larger than the other teeth in the front of the mouth. In a group of animals known as rodents—rats, mice, rabbits, and beavers—the upper and lower central incisors are used for gnawing and cutting. In fact, these animals *must* gnaw in order to keep those teeth worn down to size. If a rodent is prevented from gnawing, its incisors will continue to grow into such long tusks that the animal will soon be unable to close its mouth. In humans these teeth do not continue to grow, and they are used for gentler forms of cutting, such as biting off the food that we are about to chew. Because our incisors are in an unprotected forward position in the mouth, as well as thin and flat, they run a special risk of being chipped, broken, or knocked out.

On either side of the incisors, upper and lower, are the *cuspids*. These are sometimes called "canine" teeth because they are pointed, like a dog's large tearing teeth. They are also called "eyeteeth" because the long roots of the upper cuspids seem to point directly up toward the eye sockets.

The word *cuspid* comes from the Latin word meaning "point" or "pointed end," and the cuspids do indeed have a single point each. They also have a longer root than the incisors and are thicker, with a triangular shape rather than the "curved blade" shape of the incisors. We use these strong, deeply rooted teeth to cut and tear tough and stringy foods such as meats and fibrous plants. In cats, dogs, wolves, and bears these canine teeth are much longer and sharper than ours, and are used as weapons. In humans these teeth are the evolutionary remains or vestiges of teeth that were much larger, longer, and sharper in our ancient ancestors.

Next to the cuspids, and halfway around the jaw on each side, top and bottom, are the *premolars*, or *bicuspids*. They usually have two sharp points, or cusps, side by side. These teeth occur only in the permanent crop of teeth; there are none among the baby teeth.

(1 4)

The bicuspids are chunky teeth with heavy roots for firm anchoring in the jaw, and with a deep cleft or valley between the two cusps. When these teeth come in properly, the cusps and valleys of the upper and lower teeth fit very neatly and tightly together when we bite down. Dentists speak of the fit of upper and lower teeth together as *occlusion.* The main function of the bicuspids is to crush and squeeze large chunks of food into smaller chunks, and to punch the food full of holes so that it can be more easily ground up by the molars prior to swallowing. They also help us to gnaw bone, gristle, or fibrous plant foods. The bicuspids will usually remain more sharply pointed throughout life than any of the other teeth.

Finally, farther back in the jaw, top and bottom, are the heavy *molar* teeth. The molars are the "work horses" of our chewing system. They are large, thick, comparatively flat grinding teeth, with roots set deep into the jawbones for stability. These teeth must be strong enough to transmit the enormous force of the powerful jaw muscles, which can—believe it or not—produce a crushing pressure up to 25,000 pounds per square inch! The molars not only meet in up-and-down chewing motions, but also grind from side to side so that tough, fibrous food materials can be crushed into fragments.

In order to function properly for biting, chewing, and grinding, all the teeth in the upper and lower jaws must fit together, or occlude, precisely. If even one tooth is slightly out of line, it can disturb the occlusion of all the other teeth. Thus the dentist is concerned that both the first and second crop of teeth come in at the proper time and in the proper place until the first crop is completely shed and the second crop completely grown, from childhood into adolescence.

The First Crop: Deciduous or "Baby" Teeth

Like other organs of the body, the teeth begin their development very early in the life of the unborn baby. When the new embryo is only three weeks old and about ⅛ inch long, a tiny crease forms near one end, known as the *oral groove*. This groove will later become the mouth that connects to the baby's digestive tract. Three weeks later, when the embryo is less than ½ inch long, several little round thickenings have begun to form at different points along each primitive jaw—the *tooth germs* or *buds* that are the first sign of beginning teeth.

Three months later, when the embryo is 7½ inches long, twenty distinct tooth buds have formed, ten in each jaw. Already calcium is being laid down to form a hard crown tip around each of these primordial teeth. By the time the baby is born, the twenty teeth of the first crop—the baby teeth—are all partially formed beneath the gum line; and some of the teeth of the second crop—the permanent teeth—are beginning to form.

Even so, it is usually not until the newborn baby is about six months old that the first of the primary teeth break through the gums. The first to appear are the central incisors, the lower ones usually a little before the uppers.

Girls' incisors appear a little earlier than those of boys. Then, at intervals ranging from one to twelve months, the remaining teeth in the first crop appear in order from the front of the mouth backward: first the lateral incisors, upper and lower; next the cuspids, upper and lower; then the tiny first molars on each side, upper and lower; and finally, sometime between one and a half and two years of age, a set of larger second molars on either side, upper and lower. By age two and a half, the baby's complete first crop of primary teeth are present and flourishing, as shown in Fig. 1.

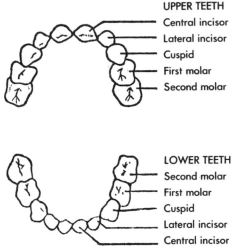

UPPER TEETH
Central incisor
Lateral incisor
Cuspid
First molar
Second molar

LOWER TEETH
Second molar
First molar
Cuspid
Lateral incisor
Central incisor

FIG. 1. *The primary teeth.*

This first crop of twenty primary teeth are sometimes called baby teeth or "milk teeth." Dentists call them deciduous teeth because they will be shed after a few years; like a tree losing its leaves, children begin losing their primary teeth when they are between four and seven years old.

(1 7)

These primary teeth are very small and very white. Their roots are short and so thus not very firmly attached to the jawbone. The thin enamel can easily fall victim to decay. What is more, the primary teeth have hardly appeared before they are being crowded from beneath by a second crop of larger and heavier teeth.

However short-lived, the primary teeth are very important. First, of course, they help with chewing. Even more, they play a vital role in guiding the second crop of teeth into proper position. If a baby tooth is prematurely knocked out, or decays and is prematurely lost, the jaw may not develop properly. The teeth on either side of the missing one may shift or "migrate" together, blocking the path of the secondary tooth underneath. Thus the loss of a primary tooth can set the stage for crookedness and incorrect spacing of the secondary teeth later, so that orthodontic treatment may become necessary. Furthermore, decay in one of the primary teeth can lead to infection in the gum or jawbone surrounding the tooth and can even damage the unerupted secondary tooth that lies below it.

For these reasons, dentists believe that the baby teeth must be protected against decay, and repaired if decay begins, even though they are going to be shed later. Most dentists suggest that children have their first dental examination at about three years old—just about the time that all of the first crop of teeth have emerged. A small amount of time spent with the dentist at this tender age can often save the child from many long and expensive visits later.

The Second Crop: Secondary or Permanent Teeth

By the age of five, a look in a child's mouth would reveal the full set of twenty primary teeth we have just described. But an x-ray would show far more. Underneath those twenty primary teeth, you would see a number of much larger teeth buried deep in the jaw—the fully developing secondary teeth, some of which are about ready to emerge. What is more, you would discover that the roots of many of the primary teeth were now either very short or gone altogether!

Between the ages of six and eleven, there is a period of "overlap" in which some of the secondary teeth are emerging to replace lost primary teeth while other primary teeth still remain in place. The first sign of this overlap period occurs at about age six with the emergence of a new set of rather large molar teeth back in the jaw *behind* the second primary molars on either side, top and bottom. These so-called six-year molars are the first of the secondary or permanent teeth to appear in the mouth. They are large, well-rooted teeth that play an important role in the further development of the jaws. Dentists call them "keystones of the dental arch" because the future growth of the jaw and proper positioning of the other permanent teeth depend upon the appearance of these six-year molars in the proper position at the proper time.

Soon after the six-year molars appear, the primary incisors begin to loosen and fall out, to be replaced by larger secondary or permanent incisors. When you look at a primary tooth that has been shed, you can see it has no root left at all. As the secondary teeth press upward against the roots of the primary teeth, the pressure results in a chemical process leading to a gradual dissolving away of the mineral material of the roots of the primary teeth. Presently those teeth become completely detached from the jaw and then finally fall out with little or no pain, distress, or bleeding. Once they are gone, the larger permanent teeth underneath them soon appear.

Before the permanent incisors finally appear, however, a child often goes through a characteristic "gap-toothed" period in which all four of the upper incisors are gone, and maybe some of the lower incisors as well, with no permanent teeth yet erupted to take their place. When they do come in, a few weeks later, the two upper central incisors often seem extremely large, giving the youngster a temporary "Bugs Bunny grin." This is because the teeth do not increase in size with time and they will have to be appropriate for the adult head and features of the individual.

There is nothing fixed about the timing or sequence of eruption of teeth. Sometimes the incisors come in before the permanent molars appear; in other cases, the opposite occurs.

By the age of twelve the primary canines have been lost and replaced by the secondary canines. Meanwhile, beneath the two primary molars on either side, top and bottom, a different kind of tooth is about to appear: the two bicuspids on each side, top and bottom, that were not represented at all among the twenty primary teeth. These new bicuspids press against the roots of the primary first and second molars until those roots disappear and the primary molars are lost.

At about the age of twelve, another important change takes place: the emergence of a second pair of permanent molars farther back in the jaw than the first permanent molars on both sides, top and bottom.

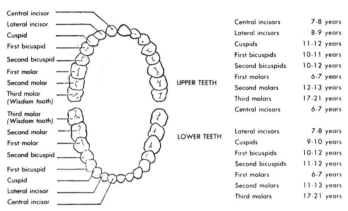

	Central incisors	7-8 years
	Lateral incisors	8-9 years
	Cuspids	11-12 years
	First bicuspids	10-11 years
	Second bicuspids	10-12 years
UPPER TEETH	First molars	6-7 years
	Second molars	12-13 years
	Third molars	17-21 years
	Central incisors	6-7 years
	Lateral incisors	7-8 years
LOWER TEETH	Cuspids	9-10 years
	First bicuspids	10-12 years
	Second bicuspids	11-12 years
	First molars	6-7 years
	Second molars	11-13 years
	Third molars	17-21 years

FIG. 2. *The adult teeth.*

Obviously there would not be room enough in a child's jaw to hold all these large permanent teeth earlier. But by the time these so-called twelve-year molars emerge, the youngster has entered a period of swift body growth, including growth of the upper and lower jaws. This growth usually makes room for these larger teeth. Virtually all of the primary teeth have been lost, and the youngster now has a new set of twenty-eight secondary, or permanent, teeth: four upper incisors, four lower incisors, two upper and two lower canines, four upper and four lower bicuspids, and four upper and four lower molars. (See Fig. 2.)

If the youngster's jaw enlarges and widens steadily as his

or her second crop of teeth erupt, and if the primary teeth are lost on schedule, as they normally should be, the youngster will end up with permanent teeth that meet together, top and bottom with normal occlusion. Sometimes, however, the jaw development is slightly slower than normal, or eruption of the secondary teeth is faster than normal, or a primary tooth remains in place longer than it should. In such cases the permanent teeth come in crowded or slightly displaced.

Sometimes heredity plays a role; a child might inherit an unusually small, narrow jaw with insufficient room for the permanent teeth. Sometimes one of the permanent teeth develops slightly out of place in the jaw and becomes jammed, or *impacted*, against another tooth as it tries to emerge. (See Fig. 3.) Sometimes a primary tooth remains in place too long, so that the secondary tooth beneath it comes in out of line. In other cases persistent thumb-sucking may force emerging secondary teeth into the wrong position.

Any such influences can lead to the improper positioning of the emerging secondary teeth. Often the dentist can spot the trouble early and take simple steps to correct it. Sometimes the trouble corrects itself as the upper and lower jaws mature. But in other cases, nature may later need help in realigning and moving these permanent teeth into their proper positions.

One final event usually occurs before the period of tooth eruption is over. Between the ages of sixteen and twenty-one, a third set of large molars—the so-called wisdom

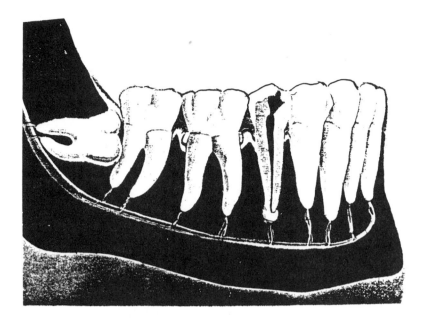

Fɪɢ. 3. *Impacted third molars may create forces that can result in serious dental disorders.*

teeth—begin to make their appearance behind the second permanent molars. These teeth, more than any others, tend to cause problems. If they emerge before the jaw has widened enough to receive them, they may be impacted against the second molars, or there may not be room for them to emerge at all. Even when they erupt in the proper positions, they are so far back in the mouth and so difficult to keep clean that they are exceptionally vulnerable to decay. Sometimes one of the wisdom teeth may never fully form at all, but may remain as a small lump of calcified tissue in the jaw which, if partially erupted, can lead to

(2 3)

decay and deep-seated infection. Sometimes a dentist can discover this kind of problem long before it actually occurs and take simple, preventive measures to help avoid trouble. But in other cases, major dental work may sooner or later be necessary.

By the time most people reach twenty-one, they have developed their all-time supply of fifty-two teeth: twenty primary teeth, used only for a brief period and then lost, and thirty-two secondary teeth which can, under ideal conditions, last for a lifetime. Unfortunately, conditions are not always ideal. A number of things can go wrong with the teeth and require later repair, correction, treatment, or even replacement. Many of these things can be prevented completely if we understand *why* they occur and what can be done to fight dental disease. Even when things do go wrong, hope is not lost. Virtually every kind of dental disease, if discovered and treated early, can be stopped and repaired before the teeth are completely destroyed. In the next chapter we will look briefly at the basic structure of the teeth, and then see how the major dental problem of young people—tooth decay—comes about and how it can be minimized.

CHAPTER
3

Decay: The Great Tooth Destroyer

The part of the tooth you see in the mirror—the "business end" of the tooth, so to speak—is only part of the whole tooth structure. Actually, each tooth is composed of three basic parts: the *crown*, the *neck*, and the *roots*, as illustrated in Fig. 4.

The crown is the part of the tooth that emerges above the gum line. The entire surface of the crown is coated with an exceptionally hard, brittle, glassy material known as *enamel*. This enamel is the hardest material in the body. It contains 97 percent glass-hard calcium compounds, with only about 3 percent organic material binding the calcium together. In fact, the enamel is not really living material at all. It does not grow and it cannot repair itself when injured. It encases the tooth crown on all sides, like a hard

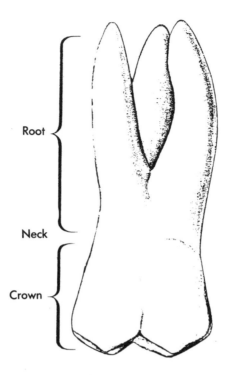

Root

Neck

Crown

FIG. 4. *Basic parts of the tooth.*

shell, and extends down the neck of the tooth to about ⅛ inch below the gum line.

Inside this enamel casing we find a different kind of tooth material known as *dentin,* softer than enamel, slightly compressible, and not nearly so brittle. Dentin is slightly yellow in color, compared to the white of the enamel. It contains about 72 percent calcium and phosphorus mineral salts and 28 percent organic matter. This means that the dentin is far more vulnerable to infection and decay than the outer enamel. Dental scientists believe that tiny

(26)

nerve endings extend into the dentin through microscopic canals. This could explain why the dentin is so very sensitive to pain, heat, and cold. As shown in Fig. 5, the dentin fills most of the interior of the crown of the tooth and also extends down into the roots. Only at the center of the tooth does the dentin give way to a hollow known as the *pulp chamber.*

The pulp chamber is the most actively living part of the tooth. It holds the nerves that supply sensation of the tooth

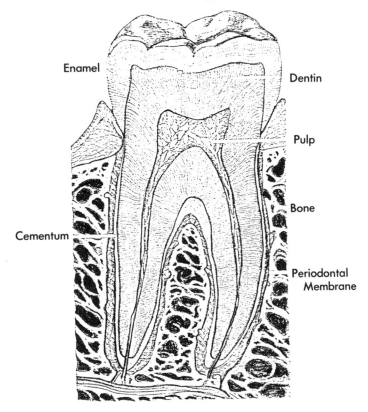

FIG. 5. *Cross section of tooth and gum.*

(2 7)

and the tiny blood vessels that carry nutrients to the
dentin. These make up the *pulp* of the tooth. They enter
the tooth at the very tip of the roots. Because of its nerves,
the pulp is extremely sensitive to heat, cold or pressure.
Some of the worst of all toothaches occur when the pulp
chamber is infected by decay bacteria.

Structures surrounding the teeth are also important to
their health and positioning. The roots are deeply embed-

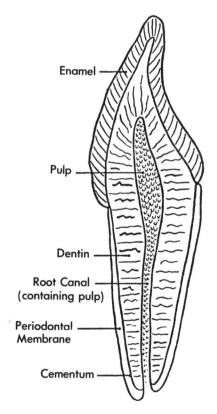

Enamel

Pulp

Dentin

Root Canal
(containing pulp)

Periodontal
Membrane

Cementum

FIG. 6. *Cross section of a tooth.*

ded in the rather soft, spongy bone of the jaw. Between the bone and the root there is a very thin membrane of cells known as the *periodontal membrane* (the word periodontal comes from two Latin words meaning "around the tooth"). At the neck of the tooth there is a thicker mass of soft, supporting tissue known as the gum, or *gingiva*. The root of the tooth itself is attached to the jawbone by means of the periodontal membrane connecting the bone and a hard, bonelike substance known as *cementum*. The cementum covers all of the roots except the tiny opening of the root canal at the root tips.

You might think that a tooth would have to be firmly anchored to the jawbone by means of some kind of solid tooth-to-bone glue, the way a chair leg is anchored into a seat. But this is not true. The periodontal membrane consists of a thin layer of living cells between the cementum of the tooth root and the bone. This provides a small amount of natural padding. The tooth is held firmly enough under ordinary circumstances, but if some unusual pressure is applied to the tooth over a period of time, the bit of padding between tooth and bone can give slightly and allow the tooth to move. If such a pressure is maintained on a tooth for a longer time, some of the bone on the "pressed" side will begin to dissolve away while new bone will form on the opposite side of the tooth.

This is a very slow process, but over a period of time it is possible to shift the position of a tooth in the jaw without loosening it from its moorings. This kind of "forced movement" of teeth can be accomplished more quickly and easily in young people than in adults, whose jawbones are harder and more fully developed. Thus it is much easier for a dentist to make corrective changes in the position of a person's teeth between the ages of twelve and sixteen, for example, than to wait until the person is twenty-five or thirty.

Plaque: The Bane of Healthy Teeth

You might think that teeth, made of the hardest and most durable material in the body, would be highly resistant to damage or disease. Unfortunately, however, the strongest and healthiest teeth have one mortal enemy constantly at work, threatening them with damage and destruction. This enemy is *plaque,* a substance that tends to form on the teeth and break down their best defenses.

What is plaque, and where does it come from? Strange to say, the mouth is one of the "dirtiest" spots in the body. Many bacteria are present in the mouth, year in and year out, living in the cracks and crevices between the teeth or lodged in the tiny spaces between the teeth and the gums. The normal body temperature and the saliva in the mouth provide a warm, moist habitat in which these bacteria grow and thrive. What is more, these bacteria are constantly at work breaking down or digesting bits of food that catch between the teeth or wedge between the teeth and the gums. These bacteria, mixed with food debris, begin to form a filmlike deposit over the enamel of the teeth, especially in the crevices between the teeth and in the area where the teeth and gums meet. It is this surface film which dentists call plaque.

What is so bad about plaque forming on the teeth? First, a little plaque leads to more plaque. The slightly rough surface of the plaque tends to hold bacteria and food debris more readily than the clean, polished enamel surfaces of the teeth. In some areas the plaque piles up, layer upon layer upon layer, forming a sort of chalky crust, called *tartar,* in the crevices between the teeth and along the gum lines (Fig. 7).

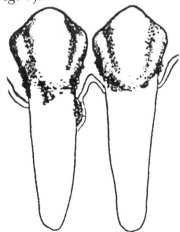

Fig. 7. *Tartar and its deleterious effects on the periodontium.*

But plaque does more than just dull the natural beauty of the teeth. It also provides a breeding ground for more bacteria, and that's where the trouble really begins. These bacteria live by digesting organic matter in the food debris lodged in the plaque. They are especially active when the food debris contains carbohydrates, and particularly sugars. In digesting sugary or starchy material, the bacteria produce acids which can attack and dissolve the hard calcium compounds that make up the enamel of the tooth. The more the teeth are exposed to sweet, sugary foods that tend to stick and cling, the more rapidly and actively these bacterial acids are formed. Dentists have found that these acids may be formed in the mouth in as little as fifteen minutes after eating a candy bar or a bowl of sugared cereal.

Of course, bacterial acid cannot dissolve away teeth overnight. What it can do is constantly eat away at the enamel, a little at a time, hour after hour, day after day. Gradually it roughens the smooth glassy surface of the enamel. Then it eats tiny pits in the surface. Sooner or later the acid will eat a tiny hole right through the enamel into the dentin beneath. This hole may be microscopically small, but it traps still more food debris and more bacteria, so that more acid is formed. Presently the bacterial acids are working on the dentin itself, and the dangerous process of dental decay is well under way.

Such areas of decay are called *dental caries.* We often speak of them as "cavities." Once a hole has been eaten through the enamel, the decay can spread much more rapidly in the softer dentin of the tooth, extending up the dividing line between the dentin and the enamel on all sides, until a large interior area of decay is produced. At this point, the damage may hardly be detectable when the dentist examines the tooth; only dental x-rays can reveal the true extent of the damage. Soon, however, the problem becomes obvious. As the dentin is eaten away, it can no longer provide support for the brittle enamel on the outside of the tooth, and bits and pieces of the enamel begin chipping off. If untreated, half the crown of the tooth may soon be undermined with decay. In some cases the tooth becomes very sensitive to heat or cold. In other cases there is no pain or discomfort at all until the damage is widespread.

Left unchecked, the decay sooner or later will reach the pulp cavity of the tooth and cause severe toothache. Once bacteria enter the pulp cavity, they cause infection of the nerves and blood vessels within it. As white blood cells try to fight down the infection, many of them are destroyed and the pulp cavity becomes filled with pus, sometimes building up such interior pressure against the nerve that an agonizing toothache results. What is more, the infection can easily extend down the root canal into the bone tissue at the tip of the root and form a pocket of pus there known as an *abscess*. At this point the pulp is dead—destroyed by decay and infection. A dentist, by means of difficult and painstaking care, may be able to get rid of the infection and restore what remains of the tooth to usefulness. But he can never bring the pulp to life again.

The Fight Against Decay

Dental decay is the most common of all dental diseases. Beginning with the formation of plaque on the surface of healthy teeth, it can lead to the destruction of an entire tooth if it is not stopped. It can happen to people of all ages but occurs most often among school-age young people. In some cases it may be a very slow process, perhaps affecting only one tooth over a period of five or ten years; in other cases it may move more swiftly and affect many teeth at the same time. No one knows why, for sure. Perhaps some people are born with harder, more decay-resistant enamel than others. Nutrition during childhood may also be a factor. Without adequate amounts of calcium-rich milk and vitamin D during the early years, the teeth may not become as healthy and strong as they should be.

One factor, however, outweighs all the others in paving the way to tooth decay: *the kind of food a person eats.* People who consume large quantities of candy, sugary soft drinks, sugar-coated cereals, and other sugar-containing foods are far more likely to have tooth decay than those who keep their intake of sugary foods down to a minimum. Carbonated soft drinks are particularly bad for the teeth. They contain not only a great deal of sugar but also carbonic acid, which in itself can attack the calcium minerals in the enamel of the teeth.

What can be done to combat tooth decay? There are several things that you can do. The best, and easiest of all, is to prevent the whole process of decay before it gets started. Remember that the first step toward decay is the formation of plaque—bacteria plus food debris—on the teeth. There is no way to get rid of all the bacteria in the mouth; even antiseptic mouth washes do not really help very much. But you *can* get rid of food debris, and thus slow down the formation of plaque, simply by *flossing the teeth* at least once a day and *brushing the teeth in the right way, for a long enough time, often enough.*

We put flossing first because most dentists agree that using dental floss on the teeth is the single most useful way to prevent formation of plaque—and a procedure that all too many people overlook. Dental floss is a fine ribbon of flax fiber that can be "seesawed" down between the teeth to remove food particles and resultant plaque from crevices the toothbrush can seldom reach. Floss comes waxed or unwaxed; either kind is spendid as long as it is used regularly. The spaces between each of the teeth require attention, and flossing after the evening meal is likely to be the most valuable in preventing plaque formation.

Why is flossing so often overlooked, even by people who want to take good care of their teeth? Probably because the process is a little clumsy and seems too time-consuming for today's impatient young people. It does require a few moments to do a good job of flossing, but one dentist has a useful suggestion. He tells his young patients to take the roll of dental floss into the TV room and floss their teeth every evening while watching their favorite show. Whenever you choose to do it, however, a thorough flossing once a day will go a long way toward fighting plaque formation on the teeth.

Brushing, of course, is equally important. Yet many people don't realize that there is a right way and a wrong way to brush the teeth. All too often they brush back and forth over the surface of the teeth a few times for a few seconds and then call it a day. That kind of brushing may accomplish something—*but it doesn't accomplish nearly enough.*

Figure 8 shows the *right* way to brush the teeth. Rather than brushing back and forth across the front surfaces of the teeth, you must brush down from the top row and up from the bottom row, from the gum toward the tip of the tooth, on the outer surfaces of the teeth, top and bottom, right side and left side. Next brush the same way from the gum to the tooth tip on the back surfaces of the teeth, top and bottom, on each side. This is a little more difficult to accomplish but is equally important. Take particular care that the brush reaches the backmost teeth, a favorite place for food particles to lodge and a place you just can't reach with a casual toothbrushing. Finally, as a third step, the biting surfaces of the teeth should be brushed back and forth.

This sort of brushing really does the job. It clears away food debris from the area between the gum and the tooth, as well as from between the teeth. Such up-and-down brushing may seem clumsy, at first. It involves a twisting motion of the wrist rather than a back-and-forth sawing motion of the forearm. But time spent brushing in this manner will clear away food debris that back-and-forth

1. Clean the outside surfaces of the upper back teeth.

2. Clean the inside surfaces of the upper and lower back teeth.

3. Clean the inside surfaces of the upper front teeth.

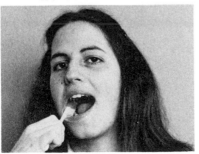

4. Clean the outside surfaces of the lower back teeth.

5. Clean the outside surfaces of the upper and lower front teeth.

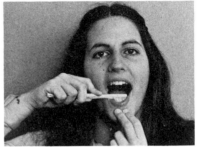

6. Clean the inside surfaces of the lower front teeth.

7. Clean the grinding surfaces of the upper and lower teeth.

8. Clean, well-cared-for teeth are an asset to health and appearance.

FIG. 8. *Correct brushing methods.*

brushing cannot touch, and help massage the gums and keep them healthy.

What about using an electric toothbrush or a "water pick" for cleaning the teeth? An electric toothbrush provides the up-and-down brushing motion with very little effort on the part of the user, and many dentists recommend it highly. (Be sure to use a toothbrush head with medium-soft flexible bristles.) It can be just as effective as a toothbrush, providing you use it long enough at a time. A "water pick," while useful in addition to brushing, can't really do the job alone. The water jet is helpful for cleaning larger chunks of food from between the teeth, but to clean off plaque most effectively, you need the scrubbing action of toothbrush bristles as well. The device should be used *after* toothbrushing, to wash away particles loosened by the brush.

How long is long enough to brush the teeth adequately? Whether you use a hand toothbrush or an electric toothbrush, you just can't accomplish a thorough brushing in less than three minutes. If you stop short of that, you just aren't getting the job done. Take the little extra time—an extra two minutes—to do a really thorough job.

How often should you brush your teeth? Your dentist will tell you that you should brush immediately after every meal and again at bedtime. That would be ideal, if you actually did it. The truth is that hardly anyone does. Most people do not carry toothbrushes to school or to work. Even if they did, they would probably not rush off to brush their teeth after every meal or snack. In fact, the "brush after every meal and at bedtime" rule may actually do more harm than good. Some people feel that the damage is going to be done anyway since they don't follow the rule exactly, so they simply don't brush at all. What your dentist may not mention is that even one brushing a day, if it is really thorough, will go a long way toward breaking up the plaque already present on your teeth and help prevent more from forming, and that two brushings a day is even better. Here, then, are some simple, practical tooth-brushing hints to keep in mind:

1. *One thorough toothbrushing a day is 100 percent better than no brushing a day.*

2. One *thorough, careful* brushing a day will help break up plaque already forming on your teeth and will help prevent new plaque from forming. Bedtime is the best time for brushing so that food particles will not remain lodged between your teeth all night long.

3. You can *double* your protection—or more—by brushing in the morning after breakfast, as well as at bedtime.

4. When you do brush, brush *long enough to do the job.* That means three minutes of brushing. Use an egg timer or your watch to time yourself.

5. Once a day, at least, use dental floss, in addition to tooth brushing, to reach down the cracks *between* the teeth and clear away debris and plaque.

What about toothpaste? From all the ads you see, you might think there is some enormous difference between toothpastes. The truth is that there isn't. Check with your dentist to see if there is one particular toothpaste he recommends. If not, pick the one you like the best. In the long run, it isn't the toothpaste that counts, it's the *brushing*. (In some parts of the country it *is* wise to use a toothpaste containing fluoride. For more about fluoride and dental decay, see page 42.)

CHAPTER
4

Enter the Dentist

Even with regular and faithful attention to cleaning your teeth the correct way, often enough and long enough at a time, a certain amount of plaque will still form on your teeth over a period of time, especially in hard-to-reach places just below the gum line or on the backs of the back molars. To get rid of this stubborn residue of plaque before it can damage the teeth, we must turn to the dentist for professional tooth cleaning from time to time.

This is an easy and painless procedure. First the dentist or dental hygienist uses a metal instrument to scrape all traces of tartar and plaque off the teeth, a process known as *scaling*. Many dentists now use a special ultrasound instrument to break up the plaque and make scaling easier. To get all the plaque off the surfaces of the teeth just below the gum line, this area must also be scaled, and a mild surface anesthetic is usually applied to the gums first to make this part of the scaling process painless. (There may be a little harmless bleeding from the gums after the scaling, and the gums may be a little sore for a few hours afterward. This is perfectly normal and nothing to worry about.)

After all the plaque has been scaled off the teeth, the dentist then polishes the enamel surfaces with a fine polishing material so that new plaque will not form so easily. Then, as a final step, the dentist will carefully examine your teeth for any sign of beginning decay.

This whole procedure is known as a *dental prophylaxis,* or "prophy." (*Prophylaxis* is just a fancy word meaning "preventive treatment.") It takes only an hour or less, and is usually relatively inexpensive. Many dentists feel that every person should, ideally, have a dental prophylaxis every six months. However, some people form plaque more rapidly than others, while some do a better job of keeping their own teeth free of plaque. Only your own dentist can tell you how often *you* should have a "prophy" for the protection of your teeth.

Fluorides and Decay

There is another decay-preventing treatment your dentist may recommend after your teeth have been professionally cleaned: the application of *fluoride* to the teeth. Careful research has shown that tiny amounts of soluble fluoride compounds taken into the body can help harden the tooth enamel and make it more resistant to decay. In some parts of the country there is enough naturally occurring fluoride in the drinking water to accomplish this goal without any special treatment. Children growing up in such areas have been found to have 60 to 70 percent fewer dental cavities than children in areas where the drinking water contains no fluorides. In many low-fluoride areas, fluoride is now added to the drinking water as a public health measure.

Alternatively, the dentist can apply fluoride in the form of a gel, directly to the teeth following professional tooth cleaning. The fluoriding tastes awful, but is a painless procedure that provides excellent protection. Finally, some degree of fluoride protection can be obtained either by using a fluoride-containing toothpaste or by taking fluoride drops. Since only tiny amounts of fluoride are necessary to harden the enamel against decay, and since the need for additional fluoride varies widely from one community to another, you should check with your dentist before using fluoride-containing toothpaste or taking fluoride drops.

Unfortunately, there has been a great deal of controversy in some communities about adding fluorides to the public drinking water. Opponents of fluoridation argue that too much fluoride can be poisonous. They worry about the long-term ill effects that fluoridated drinking water might have on the body. But medical research has shown that the tiny quantities of fluoride added to public drinking water are far too little to cause acute poisoning, and there is little evidence that long-term use of fluoridated drinking water can cause any ill effects. Indeed, dentists and physicians—the professional experts who know the most about dental health—are almost unanimously in favor of fluoridation programs. They believe that the advantages of fluoride in reducing tooth decay by as much as 60 percent far outweigh any possible harm that fluoridation might do.

When Decay Strikes

Despite the four major preventive measures we have discussed (avoidance of sugary foods and carbonated drinks, regular tooth brushing and flossing at home, periodic professional tooth cleaning at the dentist's office, and the use of fluorides), dental cavities still appear from time to time. Does this mean that you must lose a tooth that has started to decay? Certainly not. It simply means that the dentist must turn his attention to *treatment* and *restoration* of the damaged tooth.

As soon as decay is discovered in a tooth—and the sooner the better—the dentist will take the offensive. First, he will remove all the decayed area from the tooth. Then he will fill the prepared cavity with some kind of filling material to restore the tooth to its normal form and function.

The most common filling material is *silver amalgam,* made by mixing silver filings (along with tiny quantities of other metals) with mercury. When first mixed, silver amalgam is a soft, pasty material which can be packed tight into the prepared cavity. Within a few moments, however, the silver filings and liquid mercury join together, or *amalgamate,* to form a solid, hard metal filling. It remains tight-fitting against the healthy tooth beneath it. It prevents bacteria from finding their way into the dentin. In short, the tooth with such a filling has been restored to normal usefulness.

Unfortunately, silver amalgam fillings often break down after a period of five to fifteen years. They may loosen or crumble and have to be replaced. A more permanent form of filling can be made by packing the prepared cavity with successive thin layers of gold in the form of gold foil, thumping each layer down into the layer below it until the whole cavity has been filled. Applied in this way, the layers of gold foil tend to weld together into a solid, permanent filling that will never break down. The trouble is that there

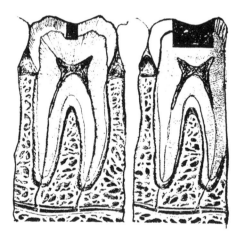

Fig. 9. *The filling of small cavities is preventive dentistry. It helps prevent the formation of large cavities, serious infection, and loss of teeth.*

(4 5)

is no quick way to produce such a filling. While silver amalgam takes only a few minutes to mix and place into the prepared tooth, a single gold foil filling can take the dentist hours to tap the material into place, layer by layer. Thus gold foil fillings are far more expensive than silver amalgam fillings.

There is another kind of permanent gold filling that can be used, however, when so much of a tooth has decayed that the structural strength of the remaining tooth is in danger. This is the so-called *gold inlay.* After cutting away the decayed area, the dentist makes a highly accurate wax pattern of the cavity to be filled. This mold is then sent to the dental laboratory. There a special plastic material is poured around the wax and allowed to set, and the wax is burned away. Molten gold is then poured into the plastic cast and allowed to cool. This bit of gold fits the prepared cavity of the tooth perfectly and is held in place by means of a permanent cement. The result is an excellent and long-lasting restoration for the tooth.

Other dental techniques are used for special cases. If the decay is in one of the front teeth, silver or gold filling material would be unsightly. Instead, the dentist may use a white cementlike material called *synthetic porcelain,* which looks like natural tooth. Synthetic porcelain has served well for many years, but this material is easily chipped and is soluble in mouth fluids, so porcelain fillings often have to be replaced. More recently, an attractive filling material for front teeth has been made by embedding micro-scopically tiny quartz beads into a softer resinous material and binding them with a cement. Such a filling material provides tougher, longer-lasting fillings than synthetic porcelain and still allows the dentist to color-match the filling material to the tooth.

In some cases so much of the crown of the tooth is decayed that the tooth cannot be adequately restored by a filling or an inlay. In such a case a tooth-shaped *crown* may

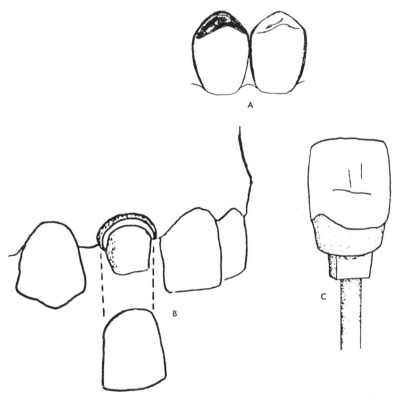

Fig. 10. *Crowns. (A) The face of this casting is veneered in porcelain or plastic. (B) Preparation and veneer crown. (C) Porcelain is baked onto precious metal thimble, which results in a stronger restoration than plain porcelain.*

be prepared to fit onto the remaining tooth. Such a crown may be partial, making up only a portion of the crown of the tooth, or it may be complete. Crowns may be made of gold or fused porcelain or porcelain fused to precious

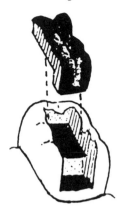

FIG. 11. *Cast gold inlay bears the stress of . biting better than silver amalgam.*

metal. In all cases the goal is the same: to stop the progress of decay, and to restore what remains of the tooth to normal function and form.

Treating Advanced Decay

When the decay of a tooth has progressed to the point that it has invaded the soft inner pulp space, repair and restoration become much more difficult. First the extent of the damage must be determined. Dental x-rays can show the dentist how far the decay has spread. X-rays sometimes reveal evidence of a pocket of infection known as an *abscess* at the base of the root, or infection of the bone around the decaying tooth. Frequently, when the pulp of a tooth has been destroyed, the tooth may turn a darker color than the others. Sometimes the dentist can observe pus emerging from the tooth. The gums around the damaged tooth may be extremely tender, swollen, and inflamed. Very frequently, such extensive decay leads to an agonizing toothache.

When such serious damage has occurred, the dentist's first task is to relieve the patient by clearing out all of the decay, including the damaged or dead tooth pulp. If infection is extensive, antibiotic treatment may be necessary or even incision and drainage of infected material. Finally the cleaned-out pulp cavity and root canal must be filled from top to bottom, and the damaged crown of the tooth must be restored.

This specialized kind of dental treatment is known as *endodontics,* a word meaning "inside the tooth." The dentist who specializes in such work (sometimes called "root canal therapy") is an *endodontist.* His goal is to preserve what remains of the tooth, by eliminating infectious matter and restoring the tooth so that it can still be used. Of course, such an extensively diseased tooth might simply be extracted—but this would mean replacing it with a false tooth held in place by a dental bridge, or else doing without the tooth. Since we have no natural replacements for any of our thirty-two permanent teeth, most dentists are reluctant to sacrifice any single one of them, and consider extraction only as a last resort.

But Won't It Hurt?

The moment we mention dental treatment to preserve and restore decayed teeth, many readers envision long, painful hours in the dental chair. Fortunately, however, the days of painful dentistry are gone forever. The modern dentist is very much concerned that his work be painless, and he has a wide selection of excellent anesthetic agents to help attain that goal.

For minor discomfort such as that involved in professional tooth cleaning, all that is needed is a simple surface anesthetic applied to the gums in the form of an anesthetic ointment or liquid. For the job of filling a small cavity the dentist will want somewhat deeper anesthesia—something like a local anesthetic injected into the gum to block the sensory nerves that supply the part of the mouth where he is going to be working. Such an injection will make the area numb for a few hours. In addition, he may use small amounts of nitrous oxide gas to help his patient relax during short procedures. For longer and more difficult work—such as dental surgery to extract an impacted wisdom tooth—a general anesthetic may be used. Whatever dental treatment you require, you can be sure the dentist will see that you are free of pain. In addition, he will use modern high-speed equipment and highly skilled dental techniques in order to make his treatment as speedy and undistressing as possible.

Today, with attention to simple preventive measures,

there is no reason for decay to progress so far that extensive dental work is necessary. Dentists will recommend filling and restoring even primary teeth that have become decayed rather than allowing them to be prematurely lost, since each primary tooth plays an important role in the development of the child's jaw and the proper alignment of the second dentition, or crop of teeth, coming in later. Permanent teeth must also be protected by *early* corrective measures to fill and restore decaying teeth before extensive damage has occurred.

CHAPTER
5
Other Dental Problems

Tooth decay is by far the most frequent of all dental diseases. But there are other dental hazards to be concerned about too. Some involve the teeth themselves, while others affect the gums around the teeth and the bone in which the teeth are embedded.

Accidents Will Happen

Dentists encounter all sorts of weird and improbable accidents involving the teeth. In one remarkable case, a young man awoke in the middle of the night to discover that his kitchen was on fire. As he rushed out the back door toward a neighbor's house for help, he forgot the wire clothesline hanging in the dark across his backyard. At a dead run he caught the wire clothesline under his upper front teeth, did a complete somersault through the air

(5 3)

around the clothesline, and landed flat on his back on the ground. By the time he reached the neighbor's house he had spat out all four upper front incisors somewhere in the backyard, and by the time the fire was out and the firemen were gone he could no longer find them. Today he has four false teeth to improve his gap-toothed smile. But if only he could have found those four front teeth and taken them to a dentist, he might today have his own teeth planted back in their normal positions again, sturdy and strong.

Most people do not have quite such spectacular accidents as this, but active young people are especially prone to having their front teeth accidentally chipped, broken, or knocked out. Strange to say, even a tooth that has been completely knocked out can, in many cases, be replanted as much as several days later, as long as the tooth is retrieved and then kept clean and moist—stored in a small plastic bottle filled with water—and taken to the dentist. But speed is of the essence; the sooner the dentist is consulted, the better the chances of a successful replant. Chipped or broken teeth are sometimes injured more severely than at first meets the eye, but can almost always be restored by preservation of the remaining tooth with a partial or complete crown.

More severe accidents—a fall from a ladder, for example, or an auto crash—may result in injury to the jaw as well as to the teeth. Any such injuries should always be treated by a dentist, or with the consultation of a dentist. Even a slight irregularity in the healing of a broken jaw, for example, can result in a small but serious misalignment of the teeth; a dentist can help ensure that the fractured bone is set so that the teeth will remain functional after healing. But the time to have such help is when the injury is fresh, not after the tooth alignment is permanently fixed out of position.

Indeed, *any* dental accident, however trivial it may seem, should be called to a dentist's attention. Even a small chip from a tooth may, for example, expose the dentin, rendering the tooth extraordinarily sensitive or painful until a protective cap is applied. Even more important, such an apparently minor injury can expose the tooth to rapid decay. A protective jacket or crown thus plays a double role: restoring the tooth to comfortable function, and protecting it from the threat of further disease.

Misgrowing Teeth

In Chapter 2 we saw how teeth normally come into their proper positions at the proper times. Occasionally, however, some factor may interfere with the proper eruption and positioning of a secondary tooth. A primary tooth that remains anchored in place too long, for example, can force a secondary tooth to come in ahead of it or behind it, so that the new tooth remains out of its proper position after the primary tooth finally lets go. Sometimes one or more of the developing secondary molars may become jammed

(5 5)

underneath an adjacent tooth so that it cannot emerge properly.

When one tooth jams against another tooth in this fashion, dentists say that it is *impacted*. Steps must then be taken either to free it and guide it into its proper position, or else to remove it. In some cases it may be better to remove the tooth that is blocking the way so that the impacted tooth can find its proper position in the jaw.

Sometimes a person's jaw is not quite large enough to allow for the wisdom tooth to come through properly, so that wisdom teeth become impacted against the second permanent molars. If the impacted tooth is left in place, it may push the second molar out of position, or raise it higher than its normal level in the jaw, so that the occlusion or "fitting together" of the teeth is not perfect. Such an impacted tooth may also cause pain and swelling due to pressure. In addition, the pressure of an impacted wisdom tooth may be transferred from tooth to tooth. This can lead to an unattractive crowding and twisting of the smaller and less firmly anchored teeth in the front of the mouth. The dentist must decide in each case, after careful examination and study of dental x-rays, whether an impacted wisdom tooth should be extracted or an attempt made to guide it into proper position.

The extraction of teeth for whatever reason is a part of a special branch of dentistry known as *oral surgery*. Some dentists have special training in the techniques of oral surgery and then practice that kind of dentistry alone. But many dentists in general practice have also acquired experience and skill in the field, and may do oral surgery in addition to other kinds of dental work.

Although a detailed discussion of oral surgery is beyond the scope of this book, one complication of oral surgery or tooth extraction deserves mention because it can be unduly alarming to the patient: bleeding from a tooth socket after a tooth has been extracted or knocked out.

As with any other kind of bleeding, the body has a natural system for controlling it. The moment that a blood vessel is broken, a long chain of chemical reactions takes place which results in the formation of a sticky, jelly-like *clot* that plugs the bleeding vessel closed. On exposed portions of the body, as in the case of a cut finger, such a clot will soon dry, shrink in size, and ultimately peel away as a scab after the cut tissue underneath it has healed. In a moist place such as the mouth, the clot that forms in the socket of an extracted tooth cannot dry and harden. Occasionally it can be dislodged, so that bleeding from the area recurs or persists.

Before any extraction or other kind of oral surgery is begun, the dentist will ask his patient about any past experience with excessive bleeding. He may also order laboratory examinations to measure how fast the patient's blood will clot. Most bleeding after a tooth extraction, however, is not the result of any defect in blood clotting. Thus, when bleeding occurs, there is no need for panic. Such bleeding can almost always be controlled in a simple way.

First, fold a gauze bandage—a packaged sterile 2 x 2-

inch dressing, for instance—into a small thick square. Place it on top of the bleeding socket, and then bite down on it to hold it firmly in place. Then sit down quietly, upright in a chair, and remain quiet and still for half an hour. This simple procedure will stop most bleeding completely, and will sharply reduce even excessive bleeding. After holding the gauze in place for half an hour, gently remove it. Then, *while remaining at rest,* wait another fifteen or twenty minutes to see if the bleeding resumes. It may take almost superhuman effort to keep from probing the bleeding area with your tongue, but this will only stir up more bleeding; keep your tongue away!

If the bleeding resumes, repeat the procedure with a fresh gauze pad for another half hour. Finally, if the bleeding persists in spite of these measures, ask your dentist for instructions. There are special materials that can be packed into the bleeding tooth socket to speed blood clotting. Alternatively, a "stitch," or suture, may have to be taken to close the bleeding vessels. But at least 99 percent of all such bleeding can usually be controlled by the simple home measures described above without having to call on the dentist.

Gum Disease and Loose Teeth

Pyorrhea is yet another kind of dental disease. This is essentially a *chronic* or long-term infection of the gums and the bone around the teeth. If untreated, it can gradually cause a loosening of the teeth in their sockets and, in the long run, actual loss of the teeth. Since this disorder involves the tissues surrounding the teeth more than the teeth themselves, dentists call it *periodontal disease* (from Latin words meaning "around the teeth"). The dentist who specializes in treating this disease is known as a *periodontist.*

Pyorrhea occurs most frequently among adults, particularly those in middle age. But the stage can be set for pyorrhea soon after the permanent teeth have emerged, and that is the time to begin preventive measures.

This disease starts in much the same way that tooth decay starts: with the formation of plaque composed of bacteria and food debris wedged into the tiny crevices where the gums meet the teeth. And like tooth decay, pyorrhea follows a natural chain of events. First, the plaque just under the gum line forms a rough surface for more food debris and bacteria to be trapped. Those bacteria not only form an acid that attacks the enamel of the tooth; they can also cause infection of the surrounding gums.

When this happens, the gums become swollen, red, and sore, a condition dentists call *gingivitis.* As soon as such an infection begins, natural body defenses arise to try to fight it down. Armies of white blood cells arrive at the scene to try to destroy the bacteria. But once the infection gets well started, it may be very difficult for the body to dislodge it.

(5 9)

As one area of infection begins to heal, another area is newly infected. Often, in the early stages, the gums in these infected areas begin to break down and bleed. Sometimes small open sores or ulcers form on the gums. As the healing and reinfection progress, the gums become scarred and begin to pull away from the teeth, thus creating even larger crevices in which food debris and bacteria can become lodged.

If untreated, this long, slow process of infection in the gums can penetrate so deeply that it invades the edges of the bone of the jaw that clasp and hold the teeth, and the bone begins to break down a bit at a time. The victim's breath becomes foul-smelling because of the drainage of pus and infected material around the teeth. Finally, as the bone is affected more and more, the teeth which were once firmly anchored begin to loosen and presently begin to fall out.

This whole process, from the first infection of the gums to the final loosening and loss of teeth, takes place very slowly over a period of years. Fortunately, this chain of events can be broken if early measures are taken to stop it. The key to prevention of pyorrhea, like the key to prevention of tooth decay, is mouth cleanliness—regular, adequate brushing and flossing of the teeth to remove food debris before bacteria can act upon them, and regular visits to the dentist's office for professional tooth cleaning. If the dentist discovers any evidence of gingivitis or early gum infection, he can take immediate steps to stop the infection before it can progress any further.

Once periodontal infection becomes advanced, however, special kinds of treatment may be necessary to cure it. In extreme cases it can reach a point at which it can no longer really be cured, but merely controlled to some extent. Such advanced pyorrhea is especially tragic when we consider that it is almost purely a disease of neglect. Simple measures of mouth cleanliness, started at the time the permanent teeth erupt and carried on faithfully, can completely control this disease. The earlier good tooth-brushing habits and regular dental checkups are undertaken, the better your chances of preventing a disorder that can lead, in the long run, to the premature and permanent loss of teeth.

Replacements and Restorations

Unfortunately, teeth sometimes *are* lost or badly damaged as a result of injury, decay, or periodontal disease. When this happens, the dentist must turn his skill to restoring badly diseased teeth or preparing false teeth to take the place of those that have been irreparably lost.

False teeth or tooth substitutes of any kind are called *dental prostheses.* * And the dentist who specializes in preparing false or prosthetic teeth is known as a *prosthodontist.*

* *Prosthesis* is the medical term for any artificial replacement part. An artificial leg is a prosthesis. So is a glass eye. In dentistry a single false tooth or a whole set of false teeth is also called a prosthesis.

(61)

False teeth today are made in many different forms to meet each person's individual needs. Not so long ago, however, false teeth were very much "in style." Certain dentists treated patients with diseased teeth simply by pulling all the teeth, good ones as well as bad, and then providing the unfortunate victim with assembly-line upper and lower dentures. Some dentists even advertised this as a cheap and permanent "budget cure" for any and all dental problems. But what a cure! Not only were perfectly sound teeth sacrificed along with the bad ones—enough of a tragedy in itself—but the cheap dentures rarely fit the patient's mouth properly, and looked as false as the wax teeth in a dime store Halloween display. Age did not seem to matter; teeth were extracted and full dentures made for teenage girls just as readily as for fifty-year-old grand-fathers.

Today modern dentistry condemns such practices. Most dentists are reluctant to extract teeth that can be saved in any way, and replacements or restorations are individually constructed.

In Fig. 12 we can see several different kinds of replace-ments and restorations. A single false tooth can be held in its proper place by means of a *bridge*, a device that crosses or "bridges" an empty space in the jaw and attaches to teeth on either side. Such a device may be constructed to remain permanently in place or to be removable. Some-times a more extensive archlike bridge can be made to support several false teeth in the same jaw. Other restora-

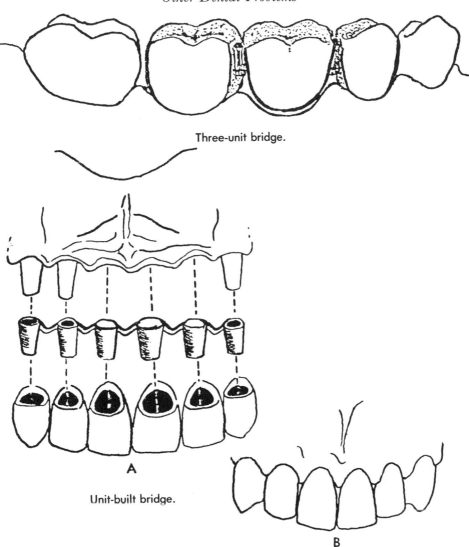

Three-unit bridge.

Unit-built bridge.

A

B

FIG. 12. *Bridges. (A) Gold thimbles cover three natural teeth and replace three missing teeth. (B) After connected thimbles are cemented, six individual porcelain crowns are cemented over them.*

(6 3)

tions involve *partial dentures*—removable devices that can hold one, two, or more false teeth in place.

For those who have no good teeth remaining at all, *full dentures*—upper, lower, or both—can be constructed. Full dentures must be carefully fitted to the individual's gums and the interior of his mouth so that they will remain firmly in place.

The dentist will help the patient decide what kind of restoration or replacement device may be best. He will consider such factors as the number and condition of natural teeth that still remain, the condition of the patient's gum and jawbone in the area that the teeth are missing, the care with which the patient keeps his teeth clean, and the cost of different kinds of restorations. Some may be more costly than others because they are more difficult to make, yet may offer special advantages that cheaper and simpler dentures could not provide. Fortunately, however, modern dentistry today can produce almost any kind of dental restoration necessary to help restore, as closely as possible, the normal function of a patient's jaws and mouth.

CHAPTER
6

Orthodontics

and Braces

There is one other major type of dental work that concerns young people especially: the treatment of malpositioned teeth. The treatment of this kind of disorder is known as *orthodontics,* from Latin words meaning straight, correct, or upright teeth. The dentist who specializes in correcting malpositioned teeth is known as an *orthodontist.*

Why Orthodontics?

For the vast majority of people, the twenty primary teeth come in at the right times and in the right places, are lost at the right times, and are replaced by the thirty-two permanent teeth in normal fashion. These permanent teeth normally find their proper places in the jaw and fit together with the teeth in the other jaw in a normal "bite," or occlusion.

Some people, however, are not so lucky. For one reason or another, one or more of their permanent teeth come in and remain out of proper alignment, so that the occlusion is imperfect. And for some, this so-called *malocclusion* is severe enough that it needs to be corrected.

Why do teeth come in out of line? Often heredity can play a part. A girl, for example, might inherit a small, narrow jaw from her mother and a tendency toward large, heavy, solid teeth from her father. When those large teeth try to find room in the girl's small jaw, something has to give. In other cases, as we have already seen, secondary teeth may come in improperly because primary teeth have not gotten out of the way quickly enough. In still other cases the secondary teeth may come in a little bit too early, or the jaw widens and matures a little too slowly, so that the teeth are emerging before the jaw is ready for them and some get crowded out of position.

External factors may also play a role. A tooth may have been lost because of an accident or dental disease, and the teeth on either side of the missing one tend to "migrate" slightly out of line. Habits such as breathing through the mouth or thumb-sucking can force the secondary teeth into abnormal positions. An impacted wisdom tooth may exert abnormal pressure on the adjacent teeth and force them out of proper alignment. In some cases only a single tooth may be slightly out of line, while in other cases several misaligned teeth may result in a severe malocclusion. In such cases, orthodontic treatment may become necessary to straighten and realign the teeth.

But what happens if this isn't done? What is so bad about misaligned teeth? Such a condition can have two major long-term ill effects: it can impair the function of the teeth in biting and chewing food, and it can impair your personal appearance. In most cases orthodontic treatment is recommended for both reasons at once. When the teeth are misaligned, abnormal pressures are placed on certain of the teeth. The jaws may not grow and develop properly. The function of chewing is impaired, and teeth subjected to undue pressures can become more vulnerable to damage or decay. In addition, crooked, twisted, or misaligned teeth are not very pretty to look at. Thus orthodontic treatment can kill three birds with one stone: it can restore the teeth to proper function, increase their longevity, and vastly improve personal appearance.

How Orthodontics Works

The need for orthodontic treatment usually becomes apparent sometime between the ages of twelve and fourteen, when some twenty-eight of the thirty-two permanent teeth have made their appearance. Since correction of misalignment is easiest when started as early as possible, the vast majority of the orthodontist's patients are teenagers. Occasionally, however, a younger child must have treatment to align primary teeth, and in recent years many adults have been receiving needed orthodontic treatment that was unfortunately neglected or passed up when they were children.

The success of orthodontic treatment depends upon two factors. First, the period between ages twelve and sixteen is a period of marked physical growth and change. Both the upper and lower jaws are growing and maturing. The other factor is that the teeth, as we have already seen, are not solidly and immovably fixed in the jaw, but rather are embedded in living tissues with a certain amount of "give." This means that when proper pressures are applied in the proper directions, teeth that are out of line can gradually and slowly be shifted into the proper position, with the supporting structures in the jaw moving and adapting with them.

The orthodontist plans his work in advance the way a general plans his campaign. He knows that it may take from one to three years to get misaligned teeth back into the proper positions. They must then be *retained* in proper position still longer, until the patient's jaws reach full maturity. If a person gets discouraged and quits halfway through treatment, all the time and effort that went in up to that point could well be completely lost. Thus the orthodontist must strike a bargain with the patient right from the start: stick with the job all the way, or not at all.

With that agreed, the orthodontist then must learn everything he can about the positioning of all the teeth in the patient's jaw. Careful dental x-rays provide a great deal of information. A working model of the patient's upper and lower jaws and teeth in their "starting alignment," made out of plaster of Paris, may be helpful. In some cases certain preparatory work must be done before the orthodontist can begin. An impacted molar may have to be removed, or a remaining primary tooth extracted. If the orthodontist foresees serious crowding of the teeth in a small, narrow jaw, he may decide that certain of the secondary teeth—some of the bicuspids, for example—must be removed in order to provide room for the more important molars or to provide space to straighten crowded incisors.

Once this preparatory work is done, orthodontics becomes a delicate engineering task. If the orthodontist is to move a tooth, slowly and gently, out of its present improper position in the jaw and into the right position, he must first have some kind of an anchor, something to pull against. He must also have firm attachments to the teeth that he wants to move. Generally this is accomplished by cementing braces to the teeth. These braces are equipped with carefully positioned projections onto which wire or elastic bands can be looped or attached.

In some cases the braces are all confined inside the mouth and the large, solid molar teeth are used as anchors toward which to draw the teeth to be moved. In other cases the head or neck must be used as the anchor, with a strong, external metal arch used to transmit the force from the unmoving head or neck to the slightly movable tooth inside. Of course, the appliances inside the mouth provide many new cracks and crevices to trap food debris and allow decay-causing bacteria to grow, so special care must be taken to keep the braces clean. When the orthodontist says, "Brush your teeth after every meal and at bedtime," he means it! He knows that tooth decay is a constant danger which can threaten the results of his treatment at any time.

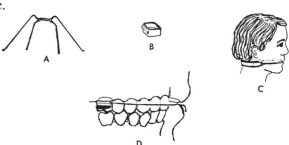

FIG. 13. *Orthodontic devices. (A) Arch wire and yolk to be used with occipital strap; (B) Molar orthodontic band with tubes to accommodate arch wires; (C) Occipital anchorage strap (neck band); (D) Interior appearance of the occipital arch wire fitting with tube on molar band.*

Placing the braces is just one step in a long process of tooth straightening. Teeth must not be moved too far too fast; they must be gently eased into proper position, a little at a time over an extended interval. During this time, repeated visits to the orthodontist are needed so that pulling wires can be tightened, tiny screws advanced a little at a time, elastic bands tightened or loosened, and the progress of the tooth movement carefully checked. A missed appointment can mean that a certain tooth is pulled a trifle farther than it should be, so that additional time must be devoted to pulling it back again. Although there is occasionally some discomfort in the beginning, when unfamiliar pressures are first applied to the teeth, the vast bulk of orthodontic treatment is quite painless—but, on the other hand, it must be endured for a prolonged period.

The Patient's Part

There is probably no other kind of dental treatment in which success depends so much on the patient himself. And you, as the patient, must put up with double trouble. You not only have the discomfort of a mouthful of appliances to keep clean, but must also face the distress of having your appearance marred by the brace head gear, or guide wires. If you feel that this is a greal deal for anyone to have to endure, you are perfectly right—and unfortunately, there is not much you can do except to endure it. Braces are not very attractive, never have been, never will be. You can, however, take heart from one fact: you will not be the only one wearing them. The need for orthodontic treatment is frequent enough so that some of your friends and classmates will be enduring the same anguish at the same time that you are.

And slow as it may seem, the time will pass and you will begin to realize that the braces were not in vain. You are simply paying now for future benefits—and the benefits are worthwhile. Spending two years in braces at this point in your life will improve your appearance, add to your comfort in using your teeth, and contribute to your overall dental health for the rest of your life.

Finally, you will gradually come to realize that other people really do not notice your braces nearly as much as you imagine they do. In fact, many of your apprehensions about your appearance will be mostly in your own mind, not in the minds of others. And at last, like the man who hit himself in the head with a hammer because it felt so good when he stopped, you will reach that glorious day when the band remover is applied and the appliances are removed, leaving you with a fine set of perfectly aligned and healthy teeth.

Removal of the braces is an important goal, but the job is not yet finished. Teeth that have been moved can move back again. Progress that has been made can be lost. Thus you will begin a second and vital phase of orthodontic treatment, that of holding or *retaining* your teeth in the position the orthodontist has achieved until your jaws have reached full growth, maturity, and development.

In most cases the orthodontist will provide you with a *retainer*—a removable mouthpiece formed for your teeth in their proper position. You will be asked to wear the retainer for a certain amount of time each day in order to hold your teeth in their new positions until they become well fixed and the growth changes in your jaw come to an end. Usually you can do this by wearing the retainer at odd hours, while you are studying or at night while you sleep.

Continuing visits to the orthodontist will be necessary during this interval so that he can check that your teeth are being retained in the proper position. These visits will not be as frequent as during the active re-positioning process, but they are every bit as vital. Far too many young people who reach this point in their orthodontic treatment get disgusted and want to quit. But after you have gone through the long period with the braces on, it doesn't make sense to risk losing what has been gained at this late stage of the game. The minor inconvenience of wearing a retainer for a period of time each day is a small price to pay for holding on to the benefits you have already earned.

The teeth are a vital part of the healthy human body, important for the full enjoyment of food and for preparing food for the process of digestion. In addition, they are an important part of your appearance and your smile. Like other parts of the body, teeth can fall victim to a variety of disorders and diseases—yet simple, commonsense preventive measures, if taken in time, can stop most dental problems from arising.

The preventive rules are both easy and inexpensive to follow. Good habits of dental hygiene are easy to acquire and easy to maintain; they require only a few minutes of your time each day and a small amount spent each year for toothbrushes, toothpaste, and dental floss. A few dollars spent each year to visit the dentist for prophylaxis and preventive maintenance *before* dental diseases have begun can save hundreds or even thousands of dollars later. When dental treatment does become necessary, it can be performed quickly, painlessly, and with a high degree of professional skill. With the resources your dentist has to offer, plus a small amount of commonsense attention to the care of your teeth at home, there is no longer any need to suffer extensive or destructive dental disease. Your teeth will give you a lifetime of faithful and flawless service—if you let them.

Index